This book belongs to

....

....

To my daughters Vanessa, Anouk and Kianna.
In memory of our beloved dog Ricky.

Special thanks to my friend - Illustrator Muthuhari.

First paperback edition December 2020

Illustrations by Muthuhari Attanayake

ISBN 9798589078565

Published by Amazon.com

The New Dog

Written By Isabelle Guérette

Zaza was going to grandma Vivi's house.

As soon as she arrived...

...a dog jumped on her
and licked her face wet.

"Zaza, meet your new
four-legged friend!"

said Grandma Vivi.

"Do you want to help me pick
a name for him?"

Zaza was so happy!

Grandma bought a dog

and waited for her to choose his name.

"Oh, yes! Thank you very much,
Grandma Vivi."

Naming a dog is an important task!
thought Zaza.
What name would fit this long,
yet short creature?

"I know, Pickle!"

shouted Zaza.

"I want to call him Pickle!"

The new dog ran up the stairs, stopped in front of Zaza, and barked at her while wagging his tail.

"Well, I think Pickle just agreed with your choice, my love",

Grandma Vivi said joyfully.

"I'm going to take good care of you Pickle!"

Zaza said.

After a minute of thinking, she asked Grandma Vivi,

"Grandma, how do we take care of a dog?"

Looking tenderly at Zaza,
Grandma Vivi answered,

"Dogs need to be fed doggy food
and given clean water
to drink every day."

"I can do that!"
said Zaza proudly.

"They also need to be bathed,
petted
and given a lot of love"

"I can do that!"

"They need a lot of exercise, so we need to take walks and play with them every day",

Grandma said.

"I can do that!"

"When they go poo, we need to pick it up with a little bag and then toss it in the garbage."

"Yarky! I don't think I can do that!" Zaza said.

"Don't worry, my love!" answered Grandma Vivi.

"Until you get used to it, I'll be right there with you to walk Pickle".

"Thank you Grandma Vivi!
Oh, Pickle!
You're going to be my

best friend!"

THE DOGGY QUIZ
(True or False)
*The answers are on the next page

Questions:

1. Dogs are colorblind and can only see in black and white.

2. Dogs can dream during their sleep.

3. Dogs sweat from their mouth and body.

4. Dalmatian puppies are born without their black spots.

5. Dogs can hear four times as far as humans.

6. Dogs have ten different muscles they use to move their ears.

7. Dogs have a superior sense of smell to humans.

8. Every dog has a unique nose print.

9. Dogs can eat everything humans eat.

10. Dogs have the intelligence of a two-year-old child.

THE DOGGY QUIZ
(Answers)

1. **False:** Dogs can see colors. Since they only have 2 types of cones (photoreceptors) in their eyes, they can't see the difference between red and green. Humans have 3 types of photoreceptors, and dragon-flies have 20. Wow! Imagine that!

2. **True:** Just like us, dogs can dream during their sleep.

3. **False:** Dogs only have sweat glands on the pads of their paws and their noses. We humans have sweat glands all over our body.

4. **True:** Dalmatian puppies are born white. The spots start appearing at three to four weeks of age.

5. **True:** Dogs have very good ears. They can hear a sound four times further away than humans can and ten times more accurately.

6. **False:** Dogs have 18 muscles in their ears. They use their ears to communicate in the same way humans use their face muscles for facial expression.

7. **True:** Dogs can smell way better than us. In fact, their sense of smell is a million times better than ours.

8. **True:** Every dog has a unique nose print, just like humans have unique fingerprints.

9. **False:** Like us, dogs can eat meat and most fruits and vegetables, but they can't eat grapes, garlic, onions, or chocolate. These foods are very dangerous for their health.

10. **True:** Dogs are as smart as a two-year-old, and they love to learn. They can understand about 150 words and gestures.

Printed in Great Britain
by Amazon